CW01020361

Swinging BRITAIN

Fashion in the 1960s

Mark Armstrong

Published in Great Britain in 2014 by Shire Publications Ltd,
PO Box 883, Oxford, OX1 9PL, UK.

PO Box 3985, New York, NY 10185-3985, USA.

E-mail: shire@shirebooks.co.uk   www.shirebooks.co.uk

A CIP catalogue record for this book is available from the British Library.

Shire General no. 009.   ISBN-13: 978 0 74781 248 7

Mark Armstrong has asserted his right under the Copyright, Designs and
Patents Act, 1988, to be identified as the author of this book.

Designed by Tony Truscott Designs, Sussex, UK
and typeset in Bembo and Helvetica Neue.

Printed in China through Worldprint Ltd.

14 15 16 17 18   10 9 8 7 6 5 4 3 2 1

Cover image:
Twiggy: one of the icons
of 1960s British fashion.

Acknowledgements:

Illustrations are
acknowledged as follows:
Alamy, page 16; Author's
collection, pages 19, 44,
55, 56, 57; Getty Images,
pages 38 and 40; Mary
Evans, pages 17 and 58.
The remaining images,
including the front
cover, are courtesy of
Rex Features.

Contents

Introduction   4

The New Affluence   8

Pop Fashion   22

Shopping in the Sixties   40

The Swinging Years   58

Counterculture Revolt   74

Conclusion   92

Further Reading   94

Index   95

Introduction

THE EMPHASIS THAT British culture placed on youth, pleasure and consumption in the 1960s would leave an indelible mark on social mores and popular taste, and it stands as the most visually exciting decade in the history of twentieth-century Britain. The art, design, music and fashion of the period continue to elicit a potent nostalgia, not least for the new social and cultural freedoms they embodied. But the 1960s are also the most mythologised of decades; the 'Swinging Sixties' were certainly not experienced by everyone – even the definition of youth was highly variable according to class, gender and geography – and, in attempting a neat classification of social and cultural history by decades, the 1960s cannot be entirely isolated but have to be understood as a significant crossroads for a post-war society still in search of a better future.

The greater affluence of the 1960s was determined by the economic turnaround of the latter years of the 1950s, after more than a decade of austerity, while its radical politics, particularly feminism, did not leave any real impression until the 1970s. But fashion in 1960s Britain was representative of

Opposite:
The 1960s brought colour, vitality and a sense of freedom to British fashion and youth culture. Here the iconic Routemaster bus is used as a mobile boutique by Birds Paradise.

Young mods with a scooter, the symbol of their sense of freedom.

just how accelerated cultural change could be; it symbolised the optimism and entrepreneurship of the 'baby-boomer' generation as it came of age, its colourful inventiveness in vibrant relief against those earlier privations; and the British fashion industry – and many of the creative industries with which it was now implicated, particularly music – found a new international attention and eminence.

The initial tremors of what would become the 'youthquake' of the 1960s came with the emergence of the teenager in the previous decade. Incarnate in Britain first as the Teddy boy, the teenager was a symbol of the growing distinction between the generations, and with increased economic means, in a time of almost full employment, teenagers were identifiable as a lucrative consumer market. But it was their peers who gave young people what they wanted, and a new breed of designers and retailers was soon at the helm of British fashion. When twenty-one-year-old Mary Quant opened her first boutique, Bazaar, in 1955, in the King's Road, London, she established something of a template for other young designers, however quixotic. Quant had much of the stock made up overnight in her Chelsea bedsit, ready for the next day, and bought fabric by the yard from Harrods.

Such youthful enterprise would later pulsate through Carnaby Street and its independent boutiques, and the most remembered face of British fashion in the decade, Twiggy, began her modelling career when she was only sixteen.

The pace and experimentation that were now driving fashion echoed the desire of young people for change; for many, their lives would be very different from those of their parents, and in 1960s Britain fashion would reflect social and cultural change in an unprecedented way. While comparisons with the 1920s can sometimes be made – between the young Flapper freed from restrictive dress, wearing makeup and bobbed hair, and the young urbane independent woman in her Quant mini-skirt – the 1960s were singular in the opportunities and choices they provided young people. While there were certainly ambiguities – for instance, in regard to the 'permissive' 1960s, marriage was not as instantly unfashionable among young people as is often thought – this was, most particularly, a decade in which the extraordinary changes in fashion and style, and in attitudes towards the body, expressed shifting concepts of individuality and identity in a newly consumerist culture.

Twiggy, with her own range of mini-dresses.

The New Affluence

THE 1960s were ushered in with much media reflection on the affluence that was now apparent in Britain. In September 1959 the 'society' magazine *Queen* ran a feature entitled 'Boom', in which the journalist asked, 'When did you last hear the word austerity?' and suggested there was more money in Britain than ever before. The country was said to have 'launched into an age of unparalleled lavish living. It came unobtrusively. But now, you are living in a new world.' Citing a comprehensive set of economic facts and figures, the article claimed that Britain was the world's largest importer of champagne, that advertising was growing more than ever, and that no other retail trade had expanded quite so massively as hairdressing. Britain was, it seemed, becoming a nation of consumers; self-indulgence and the pleasures of spending were paramount, as the exigencies of post-war austerity and the spirit of patriotism it had elicited seemed now to be fading.

Absent from *Queen*'s article, however, was any mention of the fashion industry. Indeed, at the start of the 1960s, British fashion showed little sign of the international ascendancy it

Opposite:
Images of young people shopping in King's Road boutiques were plentiful in the media.

would soon gain, to become the arbiter of youthful innovation and taste. While Mary Quant had first set up shop in 1955, her name was not yet the global industry that it would become, and Carnaby Street was far from swinging. But the belief in this new affluence – whatever the realities of wealth and poverty in a country still much stratified, socially, economically and geographically – would dominate the culture and politics of late-1950s Britain. Prime Minister Harold Macmillan's memorable claim, in 1957, that 'most of our people have never had it so good' seemed a suitable measure of Britain's increasingly affluent society and would become the banner of the Conservatives' successful 1959 election campaign.

Though Britain's economy had not grown as fast as those of its economic rivals, particularly Germany and Japan, it was now more than ever part of a global economy, having turned from austerity to growth with the boost of Marshall Plan aid in the post-war years. With almost full employment, the increasing availability of consumer goods, and the security of the new welfare state, the division between rich and poor certainly seemed diminished, and the cultural renaissance of 1960s Britain, in which the youthful pleasures of fashion and music were central, helped forge a new national identity. Britain was in transition between an industrial and a post-industrial economy.

Incomes had not only risen significantly through the 1950s – they had almost doubled by the end of the decade –

Opposite:
Media images of men shopping as a leisure pursuit became more frequent.

but taxes had fallen. For the 'baby-boomer' generation, born during or just after the war, the austerity of the 1950s gave way, just as it came of age, to an amplified world of consumerist pleasures. Through consumption, class mobility now seemed possible, something that the image of the working-class Teddy boys had first hinted at, in their fine Edwardian-style tailoring. The very idea of 'good taste' would be challenged not only by the colourful and confrontational fashion design of the 1960s, but by the democratisation it embodied and the emboldened social behaviours, particularly of young women, that it further encouraged.

Terence Conran spoke in 1965 of how expendability was 'no longer a dirty word' in British culture, and the increasingly rapid turnover of fashions through the decade would instil in the consumer psyche an almost palpable sense of urgency, a need for the new and the novel. The production of paper dresses, to be worn once and then discarded, was in every sense the most ephemeral of trends, but was representative of a significant cultural shift; no longer did one shop with a predetermined future in mind, in which longevity was analogous with the endurance and solidity of marriage and family life; no longer did consumers have to consider the established order that a 'good' winter coat or 'best' hat symbolised.

Shopping became central to the regeneration of British culture in the 1960s, and, while the pleasures of consumption had once been the preserve of the more socially and economically privileged classes, consumer durables were now commonplace, particularly with the increasing availability of hire purchase. There was a significant growth in car ownership – it would more than double over the decade – and the character of the British high street was changed significantly by the new self-service supermarkets, often out-of-town, and offering far greater choice than independent grocers, as well as better prices and easy parking. As air travel became less expensive, holidaying abroad, particularly in Spain, became more popular. The democratisation that the new consumerism of the 1960s at least appeared to symbolise had been set in motion in the previous decade, but the term 'conspicuous consumption' was now ever more present in media discourse and engendered a certain sense of classism. The style commentator Peter York, remembering his own coming of age in the 1960s, described how the 'cornucopia of consumer goodies' that was now available was 'only contemptible to those who'd got them already'. When Viv Nicholson, a factory worker from West Yorkshire, won £152,319 on Littlewoods football pools in 1961, her announcement that she was going to 'spend, spend, spend', and the ensuing tabloid attentions that her spending habits invited, embodied for many the incautious drive behind the new affluence of the working classes. That this greater prosperity was bound with the complexities of social class was further evident in the labelling

of pop stars, models, fashion designers and photographers as being the 'new aristocracy'; even footballers were a part of this cultural shift. Until 1961, their wages were capped at £20 per week by the Football Association, only £3 more than the minimum wage. As their earnings accelerated, so too did their celebrity, particularly with England winning the World Cup in 1966. It was also in 1966 that Manchester United's George Best opened his first boutique, not far from the Old Trafford football ground. The boom in satire, in theatre and in television particularly, was the most explicit evidence of the decline of social deference in the decade, while the Profumo scandal that threatened to bring down Macmillan's government was fraught with class tensions. Lewis Morley's famous 1963 photograph of Christine Keeler was also a provocative confrontation with the British establishment and an early marker of the sexual freedoms of the decade with which the new fashions were inextricably bound.

While there were indisputable traces of class mobility in the new affluence and patterns of consumption, increased prosperity was not experienced equally across Britain; it could be mapped most obviously by region, but also by generation and gender. Penguin Books, which began the decade on trial for obscenity with its paperback publication of *Lady Chatterley's Lover* – a case much burdened with questions of social class – offered very different visions of the nation with the popular series *What's Wrong with Britain* and *Britain in the Sixties*.

Opposite:
Footballer George Best was one of the new celebrity 'aristocracy', opening a chain of fashion boutiques.

15

Photographer
David Bailey
and model
Jean Shrimpton.

In particular, the North–South divide was afforded rigorous attention; not all British cities had been regenerated since the Second World War, and many still bore the scars not only of bombing raids but also of economic neglect. The realist British cinema of the period – films such as *Saturday Night and Sunday Morning* (1960) and *A Taste of Honey* (1961), adapted from the play by eighteen-year-old Shelagh Delaney – explored the same field of social experience.

The class-ridden nature of the British media would be directly challenged by changes in fashion in the 1960s. Launched in the mid-1950s, the 'Young Idea' pages of *Vogue* represented a significant shift away from patrician models in *haute couture* and would prove critical in the careers of photographers such as David Bailey and models such as Jean Shrimpton, his girlfriend, as well as of designers such as Mary Quant and Foale and Tuffin. Even *Queen* tried to appear more inclusive and began to address its society readership in tones of increasing irony, as well as following in the footsteps of *Vogue*

Jean Shrimpton on the cover of *Queen* magazine, 1965.

with its 'About Twenty' pages. Sales of magazines, particularly those for women, had soared in the 1950s, and the 1960s ushered in new and experimental titles for younger women and teenagers. The market diversified significantly as women across social classes became more fashion-literate at a younger age. *Honey*, launched in 1960, had a circulation of 200,000 by 1966. Though the magazine placed significant emphasis on fashion, it also offered its teenage readership advice on leaving home, careers, relationships and sex; the magazine gave insightful discussion when the contraceptive pill was made available. Such candidness was also evident in *19*, which ran cover stories such as 'Where have all the virgins gone?' While *Honey* was monthly, *Petticoat*, launched in 1966, was published weekly, and aimed at an even younger audience.

More than ever, magazines were the mediators of consumerism. The new Sunday newspaper colour supplements – the *Sunday Times* launched its in 1962, with Jean Shrimpton photographed by David Bailey on the cover, followed by the *Observer* in 1964 – were heavy with fashion features, editorials and advertising. Fundamentally, what these offered was the idea of 'lifestyle', with images of almost unobtainable perfection and chic. Although their glossy lavishness had its influence, it was newspapers that had the greatest currency for the fashion-conscious youth of the period, notably the *Daily Mirror*, with its increased coverage of fashion and pop music. The first success for Biba, in 1964, came when the

Daily Mirror featured a pink gingham dress for mail order. They had received four thousand orders by the next day, with seventeen thousand total sales.

In 1960 British teenagers were said to have spent £850 million on fashion and entertainment, from records to cinema-going. This was the same year that National Service ended – the last cohort of conscripts would leave the services in 1962 – and such factors would determine the growth of that figure through the decade. While the new consumerism was certainly not confined to Britain alone, the very fashionableness of shopping was increasingly evident in its culture and media. The fashions of the 1960s are perhaps the most potent reminder of the social and cultural change the decade fostered, being testament to a consumer culture that grew up in a hothouse of innovation and exploration, a world in which material wealth was more democratically experienced than ever before. This at least appeared to be an economic golden age; it saw work for all, better housing and education, and improved health. In this more inclusive society, upward mobility was

Easy-care synthetic fabrics were highly suited to the new psychedelic colours and patterns.

increasingly possible. But at a time of such domestic prosperity, Britain was politically preoccupied with its simultaneous decline as a world power, most particularly through its loss of empire, as colonies were given independence, while increased immigration elicited significant anxieties. Though these and some considerable economic problems would dominate the Labour government that was in office from 1964 until 1970 – the climate of 'boom and bust' forced it to devalue the pound in 1967 – the national identity that Mary Quant and the Beatles represented was bound with the hopes of Prime Minister Harold Wilson for a Britain in which youthful optimism and industry could flourish. The first 'mods' had embodied such hopes: style-conscious, working-class young men, smart in their European tailoring, their affluence was born of the generational shift from blue-collar to white-collar jobs – from manual labour to clerical work in the new businesses and offices of revitalised British cities. Their Vespa scooters symbolised the new mobility.

Britain's reputation for innovation was now most manifest through fashion, but the defining trend of the 1960s would affect the economy in a most unexpected way. In order that children's wear might be exempt, the 12.5 per cent purchase tax on skirts applied only to those that measured 24 inches or more from waist to hem. The mini-skirt was often as short as 13 inches, and in 1966 Biba sold, very successfully, a stretch-jersey skirt that, having shrunk after manufacture, measured only 10 inches.

Opposite:
While young women embraced the rising hems of the decade, these could still provoke the censure of the establishment, particularly schools and colleges, where fines were often imposed.

Pop Fashion

THOUGH THE 1960s are most strongly associated with the music of the Beatles and the Rolling Stones, the best-selling singles artist of the decade was Cliff Richard, and the best-selling album *The Sound of Music* soundtrack. Despite the relative conservatism of British tastes that this suggests, youth identity was made more cohesive through the pop music of the decade, something in which radio and television played a significant part. BBC Radio One did not begin until 1967, following the closure of offshore pirate stations such as Radio Caroline and Radio London, which had been the main source of pop music for British listeners, but television shows such as *Ready Steady Go!*, broadcast on ITV from 1963 to 1966, revealed fully the 'mod' vitality in seaming together music and fashion. The manufactured pop idols who had enjoyed great success in the 1950s – most of whom had come from the United States – were being displaced by the more 'beat' oriented home-grown bands, and *Ready Steady Go!* was seminal to the success of many of these, as well as launching the careers of artists such as Donovan, and giving

Opposite:
Pop star Sandie Shaw's style was relatively attainable.

Cathy McGowan, presenter of *Ready Steady Go!* The show provided a stage for both pop music and fashion.

Jimi Hendrix his first British television appearance. The show went out on Friday evenings, opening with the line 'The weekend starts here'. Its producer, Vicki Wickham, was for some years the manager of Dusty Springfield, and also fashion editor at *The Mod* magazine. The show was never broadcast in the United States, but its reputation was such that *RSG! USA!* was launched in 1964 by Dick Clark, though because of trademark infringement it was short-lived.

While the host, Keith Fordyce, was an 'old school' television presenter, a seeming relic among the show's youthful bands and studio audience, his co-presenter, Cathy McGowan, was soon an icon of youth style. Recruited as a 'typical' teenager, nineteen-year-old McGowan's enthusiasm for all things pop was palpable, as was her inexperience as a presenter, but this only added to the edge that she brought to the show. The presenters would describe in detail the fashions worn by the bands, and the studio audience was carefully selected according to both fashion sense and dancing talent; tickets declared boldly, 'You have been chosen to dance on *Ready Steady Go!*' McGowan was cited as an influence by the young Twiggy, and was among the first young women in the media to wear the mini-skirt, as well as being a regular and well-reported customer of Biba. Through Cathy McGowan Enterprises, she launched her own fashion range, working with brands such as Lee Cooper, Dannimac Rainwear and British Home Stores – ventures that were vital in the national

dissemination of the 'London look' that she represented. There was even a Dansette record player produced in her name, as well as cosmetics. With these commercial endorsements, McGowan set a trend among young female celebrities and pop stars that would continue through the decade and beyond.

The mod style of *Ready Steady Go!* could have seemed redundant among the psychedelia of the later 1960s, and the show was at the height of its popularity when it was cancelled in 1966. McGowan's influence continued for some years though, as did her name as a fashion brand. The show's main competitor was the BBC's *Top of the Pops*, first broadcast in 1964 and featuring all-male presenters. The young fashion model Samantha Juste, playing the occasional role of 'disc girl', brought some sense of fashion to the show, though nothing that could match the cutting-edge cool of McGowan.

Sandie Shaw won the Eurovision Song Contest in 1967 with 'Puppet on a String', holding the number one spot on the British charts for several weeks. Known for her barefoot performances and married for some years to designer Jeff Banks, Shaw was a significant fashion influence; she would shop at middle-market boutiques that made her look relatively accessible, and she launched her own fashion label in 1968, while the elaborate beehive hairstyles of singers such as Dusty Springfield were one reason why women were spending more time at the hairdressers.

Opposite:
Dusty Springfield. Her signature beehive hairstyle and 'panda' eye makeup were widely imitated.

Ready Steady Go! had gained its highest ratings when the Beatles performed and were interviewed on the show in 1964. The band was now established as the leading British group of the decade, leading what was termed the 'British invasion' of the United States, and would remain at the forefront of fashion for much of the decade. They worked closely with designers and tailors during each phase of their career, using fashion to complement the direction of their music. In the United States, the Beatles' style paved the way for an influx of British designers; John Lennon was particularly disparaging about American fashion, suggesting that it was at least five years behind British youth style.

The band's early image had been influenced by the Teddy boy style, but the suited and booted look they later adopted gave a greater sense of unity to the band and labelled them as the popular face of mod. Known as 'the Beatles' tailor', Soho-based Dougie Millings worked with several British pop stars in the early 1960s – including Adam Faith, Tommy Steele and Cliff Richard – and designed the collarless suits that the Beatles wore on their first American tour in 1964. Millings would be responsible for

Opposite:
The Who performing on *Ready Steady Go!*

The Beatles, 1963, in their Dougie Millings tailoring.

hundreds more of the band's outfits and was given the role of the frustrated tailor in their film *A Hard Day's Night*. What came to be known as the 'Beatle boot' was a traditional ankle-length Chelsea boot with a raised Cuban heel and pointed toe; four pairs were commissioned by their manager, Brian Epstein, from theatrical footwear manufacturer Anello & Davide, to complement the band's new matching, tailored image. Anello & Davide found a new clientele and the style was soon much imitated.

The 'mop-top' haircut that the Beatles wore was collar-length at the back, over the ears at the sides, and with a straight fringe – a more European style that was a point of endless fascination for the media, and widely copied worldwide between 1964 and 1966; there were even wigs manufactured in imitation of the look. While the style was provocative enough in Britain and the United States, in the Soviet Union it was regarded as particularly insubordinate – there were stories published of young men being arrested and forced to have their hair cut to a more acceptable length. On the cover of their 1967 album *Sgt. Pepper's Lonely Hearts Club Band*, illustrated by pop artist Peter Blake, the band dressed in military tailoring, all four wore moustaches, and John Lennon began to wear his signature round 'granny' glasses – a look that revealed the influence on the band of psychedelia and the countercultural style of dressing, as well as marking a significant departure in their musical style. The band now helped

Opposite:
The Beatles in 1966, in the less uniform style that they had then adopted.

31

popularise brighter colours and paisley and floral patterns for men, while their interest in Indian culture, following their much publicised trip to Rishikesh in 1968, encouraged a trend for sandals – a style of footwear that had long been seen as effeminate in men.

Opposite:
The Beatles' Apple Boutique, 1967, with its psychedelic frontage.

Psychedelia showing its influence on the Beatles in 1967.

33

In 1967 the Beatles opened the Apple Boutique in Baker Street, London, the first of what was planned to be a national chain. The Beatles gave the Dutch design collective The Fool £100,000 to design the interior and much of the merchandise, and the store opened with much media hype, with Lennon and George Harrison in attendance. A psychedelic mural designed by The Fool was painted across the building's facade, though this soon had to be removed. The location proved to be too remote from the centres of fashionable London, and the venture proved disastrous financially, closing after only seven months. While their incursion into retail may have been disappointing, the Beatles' influence on fashion in the decade was incontestable; Lennon himself suggested that they 'changed the hairstyles and the clothes of the world'.

The Rolling Stones, formed in 1962, were promoted as less clean-cut than the Beatles, something that the media were keen to overstate. Provocative headlines, such as 'Would you let your daughter marry a Rolling Stone?', were in fact instigated by the band's manager, Andrew Oldham, former publicist for the Beatles. It was necessary that the band's styling corresponded with this image. Far more than the Beatles, the Rolling Stones embodied the idea of revolt and protest; their music, influenced by black rhythm and blues, was more raw and more eroticised – evident particularly in Mick Jagger's style of performance. While the band had in their early days tried out the uniform tailored look, their individual tastes

Opposite:
The Rolling Stones offered a more outré, rebellious rock image.

were later brought to the fore. While Mick Jagger may have been the lead singer, it was drummer Charlie Watts and guitarist Brian Jones who led the way in terms of style, though their tastes were very different. Watts indulged a love of English classics, while Jones was very much the epitome of the new King's Road dandy. As the fashions of the decade became more androgynous, the band explored more radical styles, as well as the wearing of makeup. Following Brian Jones's death in 1969, the band dedicated their free Hyde Park concert to his memory, with Mick Jagger wearing a white tunic dress by Mr Fish, a romantic image far removed from the archetypal denim and leather rock-and-roll look that they had epitomised only a few years earlier.

The cross-class social world of the art college produced many bands in the decade, the Who being one of the earliest 'art' groups. In 1966 *Ready Steady Go!* gave them their own show, and the band proved popular among mods. Their early hit 'My Generation', written by twenty-year-old guitarist Pete Townshend, spoke of the gulf between young people and the establishment, with the infamous lyric 'I hope I die before I get old'. The Union Jack flag had become omnipresent in pop culture, an important branding of Britishness used particularly in promotional media for Carnaby Street, and indeed in many of the clothes that the Who wore. Britain had a well-established popular music press, including *Melody Maker* and *New Musical Express*, as well as a number of teenage

The Who embodied the popular face of mod and its fashions.

girls' magazines, such as *Valentine*, *Roxy* and *Marilyn*, that gave
in-depth coverage of both pop music and fashion. Launched
in 1964, *Fabulous*, its name derived from the 'Fab Four'

Decorated here
with the Union
Jack, the Mini car
became an icon
of British design
and manufacture
in the 1960s and
was often used to
accent the fashions
of the decade.

nickname given to the Beatles, offered colour posters as one of its major selling points. While the pin-up was not a new phenomenon, fan culture was taken to new heights in the 1960s, and pop music offered a soundtrack to the new world of style, with fashion sometimes its subject. In 'Dedicated Follower of Fashion', the Kinks, themselves highly style-conscious, explored the colourful world of the Carnaby Street peacock: 'One week he's in polka-dots, the next week he is in stripes ... Everywhere the Carnabetian army marches on, each one a dedicated follower of fashion.'

The Kinks in 1967, dressed in the historicist 'peacock' style.

Shopping in the Sixties

AT THE TURN OF THE DECADE, the increased prosperity of consumers was not always catered for, particularly in terms of choice, and retail was on the whole rather staid in terms of its design and marketing strategies. But the rapid ignition of the entrepreneurial spirit of the decade meant that lucrative markets were being identified. The younger generation seemed open to change of every kind, and fashion retail became implicated in a process of taste-making, from the interior design of shops to the patronage of pop stars and celebrities. Consequently, shopping became more than ever a leisure pursuit, particularly among young people.

Post-war rebuilding had seen the reconstruction of many towns and cities and the emergence of the shopping centre, the Bull Ring in Birmingham, opened in 1964 and built in the Brutalist style of the period, being the largest of these. The modernist shop design used in the regeneration of major cities and in the building of new towns placed emphasis on

Opposite:
Not all fashions of the decade were revealing. There remained a market, via mail-order catalogues and the high street, for new styles that reflected social change to a degree while satisfying more conservative needs.

light and space, creating larger windows that offered increased possibilities for display and promotion to help lure potential customers inside. Self-service was pioneered by the new supermarkets but soon spread to department stores and independent fashion retailers, but it was the boutique phenomenon that most defined the look of fashion retail in the decade; synonymous with youthful creativity and entrepreneurship, it began in London but soon reached the provinces.

Entire districts of London, offering an abundance of vacant premises and low rents, became magnets for young designers and retailers. Though Mary Quant would herself disqualify the term 'boutique', Bazaar had in many ways been the earliest example. Opened in 1955 with her partner Alexander Plunkett-Greene and business manager Archie McNair, Bazaar would influence not only the boutiques of 1960s London, but those in other cities, such as New York. Ernestine Carter, fashion journalist for the *Sunday Times,* acknowledged the timing of Quant's initiative: 'It is given to a fortunate few to be born at the right time, in the right place, with the right talents. In recent fashion there are three: Chanel, Dior and Mary Quant.' Quant described Bazaar as 'a kind of permanently running cocktail party', and it prompted a new creative glamour for Chelsea's King's Road, with its young socialites, artists and film directors labelled by the media as the 'Chelsea Set'. Bazaar became known for its artistic, often

Opposite:
Mary Quant, Bazaar, 1964. Quant's ambition and innovation reflected Harold Wilson's hopes of a more entrepreneurial Britain.

So spicy!
(but utterly sweet)
'Annabel' from Peter Robinson.
A dotty crepe dress,
restrainedly frilled, guilelessly calculated
to fit by a poetical mathematician.
While navy or black spots.
Sizes 1-15 (34½-38½) Price 9§ gns.
At Peter Robinson
and Ginger Group stockists
all over the country. Write for
address of your nearest to
Ginger Group, 96 Conduit Street,
London W1

MARY QUANT'S
ginger GROUP

More affordable than her first boutiques, Quant's Ginger Group encouraged a more inclusive market.

surreal window displays and the eclectic nature of its stock, and a second shop opened in Knightsbridge in 1957. Knightsbridge had until then been dominated by department stores that catered for a wealthy clientele, but Quant's influence was soon evident. The first to acknowledge the youth market was Woollands, which in 1961 launched its 21 Shop, an in-store boutique for young women. The buyer was twenty-two-year-old Vanessa Denza, who pursued up-and-coming designers from the Royal College of Art, with whom she would work very closely. Not all stores responded as quickly to the boutique phenomenon, however: Harrods did not open its Way In boutique until 1967.

Although Quant claimed that elitism was now out of fashion – 'in our shops you will find duchesses jostling with typists to buy the same dresses' – her market was still relatively affluent, but expanded significantly when she became a limited company in 1961. She became founder-director of the Mary Quant Ginger Group Wholesale Clothing Design and Manufacture Company in 1963, the same year that the *Sunday Times* awarded her a special prize in their first International Fashion Awards, for 'jolting England out of its conventional attitude towards clothes'. Quant produced collections for the American chain store J. C. Penney, home-dressmaking patterns for Butterick, and a hugely successful cosmetics range. With her Vidal Sassoon geometric haircut, and dressed in her own Op Art-influenced designs, Quant was the image of the woman she designed for and, although she was not the first or only designer to raise hemlines, she was acknowledged by many as the force behind the mini-skirt's success. Quant was created an OBE in 1966 and published her autobiography that same year, aged only thirty-two, the changes she had sought in how young women should be able to dress now evident across Britain and its shops. Quant claimed that where once it had been the wealthy and the aristocratic who set fashions, 'now it is the inexpensive little dress seen on the girls in the high street'.

While there was a clear modernity to Quant's work, Barbara Hulanicki's Biba, which began as the Biba Postal

As a young fashion designer, Mary Quant was much photographed at work. This image is from 1967.

Boutique in 1963, represented a more historicist approach, with its Art Nouveau- and Art Deco-inspired interiors and graphics creating an eclectic but distinctive brand image. The first Biba opened in 1964, a relatively modest store in Abingdon Road, Kensington. Biba mail-order catalogues were as successful as the London store, which moved premises several times owing to demand for their affordable and diverse range. Clothes were displayed on coat stands, changing rooms were communal, and there were no window displays, but rather tantalising glimpses of the shop's lavish interior. Biba sold a large cosmetics range to complement its fashions and was among the first retailers to allow customers to try makeup before buying. The emphasis at Biba was not only on youth, but also on the pleasures of trying out different images – the shop a vast dressing-up box.

Though occupying a different market, a similar historical revivalism was evident in the work of Ossie Clark, who worked for the Quorum boutique, founded in 1964 by Alice Pollock, along with textile designer Celia Birtwell. Quorum's sumptuous fashion shows attracted many of the celebrities of the day, including the Beatles and the artist David Hockney, whose 1971 portrait of Clark and Birtwell remains one of the most iconographic images of the period.

John Stephen became known as 'the King of Carnaby Street' in the 1960s. He began his career in the 1950s as an assistant at Bill Green's menswear shop, Vince. Stephen's first

Opposite:
The first Biba boutique opened in Abingdon Road, Kensington, in 1964. Photographed here in 1967, the model wears an Op Art-influenced jumpsuit.

47

shop opened in Beak Street, Soho, in 1956, but moved to Carnaby Street the following year. He would turn this neglected backwater into the most fashionable shopping destination of 1960s London; by 1967 he alone had fifteen shops on the street. In the early years of the decade, Carnaby Street was very much focused on the male consumer — Stephen did not open his first womenswear boutique, Trecamp, until 1965. The more outré styles of the 'peacock revolution' can be traced back to Stephen's experimental approaches to menswear. More willing to test accepted conventions, Stephen's clothes were worn by many of the rock and pop groups of the time, including the Rolling Stones, the Who, the Small Faces and the Kinks — they were frequently pictured in the media coming out of one of his boutiques. Men were now conspicuous consumers, at least in major cities, and there was great attention given to this by the Sunday colour supplements, while several men's style magazines were launched. The first British model agency to represent male and female models had been Scotty's, established in 1953, and having the young Roger Moore on its books, and in 1967 the first all-male agency was opened, English Boy, based in Chelsea.

Though Stephen dominated Carnaby Street, there were many other boutiques and designers who made it an essential fashion destination, including Foale and Tuffin, Lord John, Merc and Take Six. I Was Lord Kitchener's Valet, opened in 1966, began life as a stall selling used military uniforms at the

Opposite:
Heralded as 'the King of Carnaby Street', John Stephen created a playground of innovative, youthful and disposable fashion.

Portobello Market in Notting Hill, the name intended to conjure images of tailored Edwardian menswear, and among the shop's customers were Mick Jagger, John Lennon and Jimi Hendrix. By 1966, boutique owners on Carnaby Street were making collectively £5 million a year, and rents had multiplied tenfold.

Just off Carnaby Street, in Ganton Street, Palisades was massively successful, while boutiques such as Hung On You (see page 76) and Granny Takes a Trip maintained the fashionableness and avant-garde edge that Quant had first brought to the King's Road. Michael Fish, who had worked briefly as one of John Stephen's assistant designers, opened Mr Fish in 1966 in Clifford Street, Mayfair, selling psychedelic-inspired menswear to a wealthier clientele. Fabrics were extravagant – velvets and silks – and his colourful 'kipper ties' were particularly popular. The vibrant eccentricity of the designs was emphasised by the slogan across the shop's bags 'Peculiar to Mr Fish'.

Exciting window displays and interior decor were vital to the success of any boutique, as were young staff who were indistinguishable from its customers, a fast turnover of stock, and a pop soundtrack that could capture the particular spirit of the fashions being sold – these all brought a sense of theatre to the shopping experience. While the new London boutiques contrasted starkly with the department and chain stores that had long dominated British fashion retail, these soon enough

Opposite:
I Was Lord Kitchener's Valet opened in 1966. With a celebrity clientele, the boutique recycled Britain's military heritage.

adopted some of the boutiques' characteristics. As early as 1959, with some prescience of what 1960s retail would look like, the young abstract artist Robyn Denny was invited by Austin Reed to make a pop mural for the lower ground floor of their Regent Street store – a visual language with which it was hoped younger consumers could identify. Retailers such as Jaeger and Simpsons of Piccadilly soon followed suit in their courting of the youth market.

At the other end of the high street, shops such as C & A offered an increasingly rapid turnover of fashionable styles at affordable prices, while Marks & Spencer significantly revamped many of its existing stores through the decade and consolidated its position as a bastion of British retail. But while high fashion saw Britishness as something to be marketed, Marks & Spencer boasted in their womenswear advertising of having designers in *all* the major fashion centres of the world. There was also much emphasis on 'care-free' and 'miracle' fabrics in their advertising: Bri-nylon and Terylene were popular, as was knitwear in Orlon. The wearing of tights that the mini-skirt had ushered in meant that Marks & Spencer's sales assistants wore the ubiquitous shade of American tan as part of their uniform. For men, several London boutiques had opened branches in the provinces, for example Lord John, but the made-to-measure suit was still available on the high street, Burton being a reliable provider of quality and value, and the official tailor for the England

Opposite:
The psychedelic façade of men's boutique Lord John, 1968. With Carnaby Street's proximity to the offices of record labels and management companies, as well as the celebrated Marquee Club, bands such as the Small Faces were regular customers of the new boutiques.

World Cup team in 1966. John Collier, the name adopted in the 1958 take-over of the Fifty Shilling Tailors, provided similarly dependable but conservative menswear.

While the rail network was reduced beyond recognition in the 1960s, petrol was more readily available and was vital in the distribution of goods outside of the capital. The department store Kendal Milne in Manchester began to sell Mary Quant in 1963, while the first Topshop was opened in 1964, as a dedicated youth fashion brand, within the Sheffield branch of the Peter Robinson department store. A total of £1 million was invested in the launch of Miss Selfridge as the young fashion department of Selfridge's department store in 1966. The original mannequin that Miss Selfridge used was based on Twiggy, and among its first range were paper dresses designed by Sylvia Ayton and Zandra Rhodes. Although its very scale was antithetical to that of the independent boutique, by 1967 Miss Selfridge had concessions in many other department stores across Britain, and independent branches opened in 1969. Even the magazine *Honey* had almost fifty branded concessions across Britain by 1966.

American mass-market labels collaborated with British designers to bring 'youthquake' fashions to department stores across the United States, Mary Quant being a leading example. When the New York boutique Paraphernalia opened on Madison Avenue in 1965, it sold the imported work of Quant, Foale and Tuffin, and Ossie Clark. The space-age minimalism

Her Susan Small 'Trend-setter' beach dress in BRI-NYLON had this label when she bought it. So she knows it's ideal for holiday wear—its good looks and easy care are there to stay.

BRI NYLON

Susan Small 'Trendsetter' beach dress in stretch BRI-NYLON, four colour combinations, about 10 gns.

Easy-care synthetic fabrics dominated the decade. Dress by Susan Small.

Allusion to the space age lends credibility to the technology behind Dormeuil's Cosak fabric for men's tailoring.

of Paraphernalia's interior was in some contrast to most of the London boutiques, but the store found great success, with many British celebrity followers, including models Twiggy and Penelope Tree, and the actress Julie Christie. The company began to franchise and within three years there were forty-four Paraphernalia stores in the United States, such ventures being vital in the international propagation of British fashion.

The changes in fashion retail were represented and promoted in the British media as symbols of an apparently classless youth culture, and in 1967 teenage girls were reported to have bought almost half of the total women's outerwear sold in Britain. By the end of the decade there were estimated to be fifteen thousand boutiques across the country. Barclaycard was being advertised as 'all a girl needs when she goes out shopping': yet, conversely, home dressmaking was still popular throughout the decade, as evidenced in the patterns produced by such designers as Quant, one of which sold seventy thousand copies, with many magazines promoting home sewing as a means of attaining the boutique look. Boutiques changed the ways in which fashion was merchandised and displayed, but also the consumer experience, and this in particular determined their significance in the mapping of 'swinging London'.

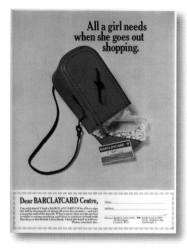

All a girl needs when she goes out shopping.

Dear BARCLAYCARD Centre,

Advertising for credit cards, now more easily available, encouraged women, especially, to spend more.

The Swinging Years

IN April 1966 the American news magazine *Time* celebrated London life and culture with a special edition that declared the city to be 'swinging'. The cover of the magazine, illustrated by Geoffrey Dickinson, articulated the colour and vitality of fashionable London alongside some of its most recognisable landmarks. Prime Minister Harold Wilson, in signature Gannex raincoat, which he had made something of a British fashion icon, waved a Union Jack flag amidst a sea of traffic that included a red Routemaster bus, a Rolls Royce and a Mini Cooper. The successful film *Alfie*, with Michael Caine, was advertised in neon lights, while the new democratisation was represented with black-tie aristocracy rubbing shoulders with a Quant-styled 'dolly bird' and an aspirant rock star – the latter wearing a Who tee-shirt and Union Jack sunglasses. In the artist's attention to fashionable detail, the concept of 'swinging' Britain was lent very definite visual clarity, with the new Britain and its 'movers and shakers' viewed not as separate from the establishment, but as woven deftly into its fabric.

Opposite:
Sunburst dress in wool crepe by Foale and Tuffin, 1965. The emphasis on youth in the fashion media was critical to the success of such designers.

That issue of *Time* magazine has proved to be an enduring document of the edge that London had in 1960s popular culture and fashion, but serves also as a reminder of the hyperbole that was needed to sustain the global distinction it had quite rapidly acquired. Dickinson's illustration evocatively captured the brash modernity of 1960s London in symbols that remain shorthand for the decade, and in her article 'Great Britain: You Can Walk Across It on the Grass', the magazine's correspondent Piri Halasz wrote how, in 'a decade dominated by youth', London 'has burst into bloom': 'It swings; it is the scene. This spring, as never before in modern times, London is switched on.' Halasz was fervent in her celebration of British fashion and pop culture and the glamorous young people at its helm, though there were readers who questioned such enthusiasm; one respondent claimed that the 'turned-on young men and women will burn out as quickly as a light bulb of British manufacture'.

With an American readership of sixteen million, however, *Time* seemed to be directly targeting American tourists. While Britain in the immediate post-war years had eagerly embraced many American imports in terms of music, film and fashion, *Time* reported on a massive cultural reversal and included a map of the 'scene' that took in Granny Takes a Trip and Biba, drawing a picture of London as global arbiter of youth style. But *Time* was not the first to suggest that London was swinging; Diana Vreeland, editor of American *Vogue*, had described the city as such in 1965. That same year, Roger Miller had a hit with the song 'England Swings'.

It was during the 'swinging' years, or the 'high' 1960s, roughly between 1964 and 1967, that a new breed of image-makers consolidated their cultural significance – young photographers who would prove critical in the fortunes of British fashion, and who gained themselves a certain celebrity. In 1964 the *Sunday Times* colour supplement, both exemplar and chronicler of Britain's glossy new style-consciousness, ran an article entitled 'The Model Makers', naming David Bailey, Terence Donovan and Brian Duffy as the 'terrible three' of fashion photography; Norman Parkinson gave them the further epithet of the 'Black Trinity'. That profile suggested how their approach towards the fashion image determined a sexually charged vision of London: 'The London idea of style in the 1960s has been adjusted to a certain way of looking, which is to some extent the creation of [these] three young men, all from the East End ... Between them, they make more than £100,000 a year, and they are usually accompanied by some of the most beautiful models in the world: they appear to lead enviable lives.' The journalist gave as much emphasis to the image of the photographers as to that of the models they worked and slept with, describing Bailey, with his 'thick black hair and large bright eyes', as 'handsome, reserved, slightly sulky'.

Bailey had worked as an assistant in the studio of fashion photographer John French before being contracted in 1960 to British *Vogue*, where his ascent was spectacular; in only a few months he was shooting covers for the magazine, and in any one year would shoot as much as eight hundred pages of editorial content. Where fashion photographers had previously been men of a more privileged class, Bailey exploited his working-class roots to his own advantage, and his playboy image meant that any girlfriend found herself the subject of much media attention. In the parlance of the time, Terence Donovan claimed that he, Bailey and Duffy strived to 'make the model look like a bird we'd want to go out with'. The photographs that made a celebrity couple of Bailey and his girlfriend and muse Jean Shrimpton, who began modelling in 1960 when she was only seventeen, were taken for *Vogue* on location in New York in 1962. These images heralded a new realism in fashion photography, with Bailey using a 35mm hand-held camera as the gamine Shrimpton wandered the city streets, without the

Jean Shrimpton became the face of 'swinging London'.

Opposite:
David Bailey.

aid of stylists or makeup artists. Senior staff at *Vogue* expressed significant concerns about the intimate relationship between Bailey and Shrimpton and the direction it gave his work, but she would become the highest-paid and most photographed model of the decade. The most familiar of cover girls, she even graced the American *Newsweek* in 1965; in the magazine's four-page profile of 'The Shrimp', she was described as 'the template from which the face of Western beauty will be cast until further notice'.

It was in 1965 that Shrimpton attracted massive international media attention when she attended the Victoria Derby Day at the Melbourne Races wearing a mini shift dress, and without the prerequisite hat, gloves or stockings – her only accessories were an ankle chain and men's watch. The relative liberalism of Britain was shown in great relief against the censure that Shrimpton received in the Australian media. The dress that she wore was mini in length only because the designer with whom she was travelling, Colin Rolfe, had limited material to work with, but Shrimpton had personified the freedoms and informality of swinging London that day and the incident would prove significant in further disseminating the style. When she attended the Melbourne Cup Day a few days later, however, following pressure from sponsors, she dressed far more conservatively in a tailored suit and straw Breton hat, as well as gloves and stockings. She was quoted by reporters as saying that 'you should dress to please

Opposite:
Jean Shrimpton and Terence Stamp. Their romance made them one of the most photographed couples of the day.

yourself', and suggested that Melbourne and Australia seemed 'years behind London'.

The relationship between Bailey and Shrimpton had ended in 1964. Mick Jagger was best man when Bailey married French actress Catherine Deneuve in 1965, the bride wearing a simple black dress and smoking throughout the ceremony, with the groom in denim jeans. Alongside fashion photography, Bailey worked with many of the decade's biggest rock and pop stars, and swinging London had already been gathered together in his 1964 *Box of Pin-Ups*, a collection of poster-prints of British celebrities that included the Beatles, Jagger, Terence Stamp, and of course Shrimpton, as well as international figures such as Rudolf Nureyev and Andy Warhol. The project reflected the significantly revised status of the fashion photographer, and the 1971 National Portrait Gallery exhibition of Bailey's work was an important retrospective of the decade's emphasis on style and image.

The fashion photographer in Michelangelo Antonioni's 1966 film *Blow Up*, played by David Hemmings, had been based on Bailey, as the experience of fashionable London became a central theme of cinema that was in stark contrast to the decade's kitchen-sink realism. The image of swinging London determined something of a renaissance in British film production, explored initially in the Beatles' *A Hard Day's Night* (1964), and followed for example by *Darling* (1965),

The Knack ... and How to Get It (1965), *Georgy Girl* (1966), *Bedazzled* (1967) and *The Italian Job* (1969). *Prudence and the Pill*, from 1968, highlighted many of the anxieties that were felt about the availability of the contraceptive pill, contemporaneous with the mini-skirt as a symbol of sexual liberation for women.

Elemental in many of the film narratives that used swinging London as a backdrop was the idea of almost effortless success; for anyone who had 'the look', it was easy to become a pop star or model, even a photographer or artist. The 1967 film *Smashing Time*, with its colourful scenes of Carnaby Street, its exaggeratedly lurid fashions, and photographers on every corner, offered a lightweight satire of the media that swelled the image of swinging London. It starred Rita Tushingham and Lynn Redgrave as young women from the North seeking fame and fortune as models and pop stars, but celebrity proves unfulfilling and fleeting, and the pair decide to return home. Whether celebratory or derisive of the 'scene', such narratives did echo something of the dream that Bailey and Shrimpton had together so fluently embodied – his working-class background, and hers as a gauche farmer's daughter from Buckinghamshire, had not in any way hindered their ascent into the highest echelons of swinging London.

Lesley Hornby was sixteen when she was discovered and renamed 'Twiggy'. The archetypal wide-eyed waif, with

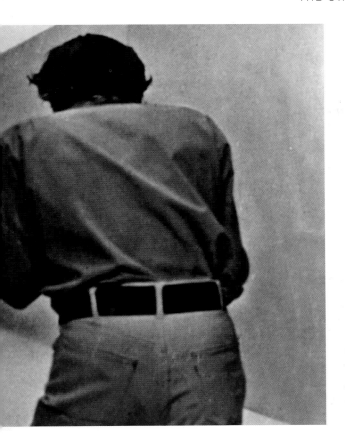

Michelangelo
Antonioni's
1966 film *Blow Up*
depicted a fashion
photographer
based on
David Bailey.

short, boyish hairstyle and exaggeratedly long eyelashes, her international celebrity was immediate, with covers for *Vogue* and *Tatler*. Twiggy's adolescent physique suited the more

androgynous styles of the decade, and she was the ultimate embodiment of youthfulness, her body keeping the demands and responsibilities of adulthood at bay. She launched her own fashion range, as well as cosmetics, including her signature false eyelashes, and even hosiery. Twiggy reflected on the culture that created her: 'I'm lucky to be young at the right time. The world is all for youth now ... because the young people have so much time and money to spend, all the businessmen say "Let's cash in on youth".'

When she visited the United States in 1967, as ambassador for swinging Britain, the *New Yorker* magazine devoted nearly a hundred pages to the Twiggy phenomenon, and she was the subject of three separate documentaries by photographer Bert Stern. The magazine *Twiggy: Her Mod, Mod Teen World* was also published in the United States, while Mattel produced the Twiggy Barbie doll. In 1969 she was the subject of one of the earliest *This Is Your Life* television tributes, despite being only twenty years old, and the following year she gave up modelling to pursue her acting career.

Only two months after that issue of *Time* magazine, *Queen* ran the feature 'Swingeing London: The Truth', describing the phenomenon as 'this plastic, primary-coloured Frankenstein thing'. Many cultural commentators were keen to suggest that the clamour of media attention was the beginning of the end for London as a capital of culture and style. But American magazines such as *Esquire* and *Life* were

Opposite:
The 1965 film
*The Knack ... and
How to Get It*
was directed by
Richard Lester,
known as *the*
'swinging London'
director.

impervious to such critiques and followed with their own profiles of swinging London, each mapping the same fashionable passage through the city. Christopher Booker's *The Neophiliacs*, published in 1969, was disparaging of the 'bewitching' nature of the Swinging Sixties and the decade's emphasis on fashionableness and image, suggesting that culture had become too dependent on the very idea of newness, that there seemed 'to be no one standing outside the bubble, and observing just how odd and shallow and egocentric and even rather horrible it was'. Even John Lennon echoed such sentiment at the close of the decade, insisting that 'nothing happened except that we all dressed up'. Certainly the image-makers of the period – photographers, film-makers and journalists – were able to represent the culture of affluence, style and youth consumerism as more colourful, exhilarating and inclusive than it could possibly be, but, however illusory swinging London might have been, it was at least symbolic of a reinvigorated Britain. Disenchantment with the world of consumerist hedonism that swinging London represented was evident long before the decade's close, though. When the first International Poetry Incarnation, held in May 1965 at the Royal Albert Hall, drew an audience of nearly eight thousand, with beat poet Allen Ginsberg as a star attraction, it was clear that the ideas of the counterculture could claim the attentions of Britain's youth.

Opposite:
Twiggy became as important an export as the Beatles before her.

Counterculture Revolt

THE MOST REVISITED look of the 1960s is undoubtedly 'flower power', and the image of the 'hippie' remains a potent symbol of how young people were politicised in the latter years of the decade. Though often used pejoratively in the media, the term was derived from the American 'hipster', and used as an epithet for the first beatniks who had descended upon San Francisco's Haight Ashbury district, home of the 'Summer of Love' of 1967. But the hippie ethos, and the image that embodied it, had significant influence in Britain in the last years of the decade, and well into the 1970s. While the dress and appearance of the counterculture were conceived as an anti-fashion statement, in expression of a rejection of all things capitalist, the image resulted in one of the most influential of dress reform movements and was soon appropriated as a 'look'.

The countercultural movement was most pronounced in the United States, where the first hippies had acquired the values of the beat generation that went before them —

Opposite:
Hippie style represented a rejection of the dictates of fashion designers.

an interest in non-Western religions, experimentation with drugs, free sexual expression, and a rejection of materialism – but in Britain there was much sympathy with the idea of an 'alternative' society, in which self-governing communities could flourish and alternative ways of living could be discovered, with an emphasis on peace and deference to the natural world. The counterculture's disillusionment with the materialism that had so much dominated post-war Western society meant a particularly virulent rejection of the mass-production of consumables, of which fashion was most representative.

While the counterculture was apolitical in terms of party politics, which were deemed to serve only vested interests, it led many issue-based campaigns. The British Campaign for Nuclear Disarmament had been formed in 1957, but the symbol that Gerald Holtom designed as its logo became, in the 1960s, a universal symbol for peace, embraced by the civil rights movement and by anti-Vietnam War campaigners in the United States. Such protests had spread worldwide, and the 1968 Paris uprising of students and workers, which almost brought down President De Gaulle's conservative government, had much resonance internationally. In 1969 John Lennon and Yoko Ono held week-long 'bed-ins' in Amsterdam and Montreal in protest against the ongoing Vietnam War and to promote ideas of world peace. There was a global spirit of revolt that expressed young people's despair with political

Opposite:
Hung On You sold an eclectic range of menswear that included expert tailoring alongside more outré hippie-influenced styles.

structures that failed much of society and, although not everyone who adopted the image would have described themselves as being a hippie, dress became both an individual and a collective statement of their discontent. At a most fundamental level, the counterculture ushered in a casualness far more marked than anything that had gone before.

In their rejection of bourgeois values and the mores of mainstream culture, hippies embraced traditional crafts and adopted a 'make it yourself' approach to dress and adornment. Bead necklaces and simple jewellery, tie-dyed tee-shirts and scarves embodied a sense of primitivism and were worn by the likes of the Incredible String Band, and could all be home-made. There was much veneration of the arts and crafts of other cultures and ethnicities, of items that were hand-produced rather than mass-produced, and which held symbolic rather than economic value. While the crafts of Native Americans were much esteemed in the United States, in Britain the cultures and traditions of the Middle East and North Africa had significant influence. There was a renewed passion for second-hand dress that long prefigured the eco-fashion and vintage markets, with fabrics often creatively recycled. It was the extraordinary appearance of hippies – an image in which seemingly disparate periods and places were brought together to produce an air of meaningful anarchy – that afforded their collective cause of peace, freedom and equality such visibility.

Opposite:
In 1967 Hyde Park in London was the scene of a 'Love-in', representing an alternative youth culture to the swinging London of Carnaby Street.

The Incredible
String Band,
photographed
in 1969, were at
the forefront of
psychedelic folk
music.

In his advocacy of psychedelic drugs, Timothy Leary
had coined the expression 'Turn on, tune in and drop out',
a mantra that was to provide a significant stimulus to the
counterculture. Tom Wolfe's influential *The Electric Kool-Aid
Acid Test*, published in 1968, and the road movie *Easy Rider*,
from 1969, each embodied Leary's proposition, and hippies

presented themselves as 'dropouts' from society, rejecting the customs of bourgeois life and conventional careers – although some would develop small businesses that catered for countercultural needs – creating a lifestyle that allowed for far greater sartorial freedom. Hair was worn longer by both sexes, its unkemptness in marked contrast with the neat, short hair of the mod look, while many men wore beards, something that for much of the twentieth century had been associated with the artistic and bohemian. Flared denim jeans and sandals were other unisex fashions, as were round 'granny' glasses, as worn by John Lennon and Janis Joplin, while the appropriation of military dress, at least initially, demonstrated a challenge to the establishment. As Leary advocated, many in the counterculture indulged in the recreational use of hallucinogenic drugs, especially marijuana and LSD, as a way of expanding consciousness, and there was an increased interest in astrology. Its symbols found their way into the hippie image, and the period was often referred to as the Age of Aquarius, something reflected in the musical *Hair*, a somewhat mediated celebration of the hippie lifestyle that opened on Broadway in 1968, and in London the same year starring Marsha Hunt, while the enormous success of the Beatles' film *Yellow Submarine* brought a psychedelic vision of the world to a mass audience.

Experimentation in music was critical in disseminating the ideas and the image of the counterculture, with psychedelic rock embraced by bands and musicians as diverse as the Grateful Dead, Jefferson Airplane, Cream and Jimi Hendrix. Of the many large outdoor rock festivals at which a number of these acts performed, Woodstock, held in upstate New York in 1969 and promoted as an 'Aquarian Exposition' of three days of peace and music, remains the most celebrated. The second Isle of Wight Festival was held only days after Woodstock and featured Bob Dylan and the Who. An audience of 150,000 was in attendance, but the following year this grew to more than 600,000 – larger than the Woodstock audience – when Jimi Hendrix, the Doors and Joni Mitchell appeared. These events were important public gatherings that were influenced in many ways by the 'be-ins' that had originated in San Francisco, and the body-painting that many in the audience wore was expressive of a sense of tribal identity, of an empathy with primitive and instinctual sensibilities that the counterculture felt had been lost in Western society.

The hippies brought a sense of lawless theatre to dressing-up that undermined the societal roles that Western dress so clearly demarcated. In their reformist capacities, the hippies underlined the ways in which dress and appearance classified the individual and imposed social barriers, particularly in terms of gender and class, the arbitrary nature of which had gone unchallenged for too long. Just as youth fashion and designers such as Quant had challenged the idea of the occasion or event wardrobe, hippies challenged the very idea

Opposite:
The rock group Cream in hippie-influenced fashion.

of seasonal collections and the culture of change that was central to the fashion system. The very fabrics and technologies that had allowed the British fashion market to expand so massively in the decade also troubled the counterculture; the use of synthetics in mass-market fashion was challenged by an emphasis on natural fabrics, and the exploitative nature of the fashion manufacturing industry was questioned. There was some evidence of a return to the values of the British Arts and Crafts movement, with a renewed interest in the work and manifesto of William Morris. Henrietta Moraes, the model and muse of the artist Francis Bacon, wrote in her autobiography of adopting the hippie image at the end of the decade, of the chrysanthemum and honeysuckle Morris print knee-high boots she wore from Granny Takes a Trip, with Afghan robes from Hung On You and 1940s dresses with lace petticoats and embroidered shawls that she found in London flea markets.

A wide spectrum of folk dress and folkloric motifs was drawn upon to create the hippie image, and the relatively unconstructed silhouette of the 1960s was made more flowing with much longer skirts in peasant styles – a lengthening of hemlines that was in marked contrast to the mini-skirt. The 'shop-bought' hippie look was largely beyond the means of those who were first drawn to the counterculture, and the threat that the hippie ethos represented – its challenge to the culture of consumerism and expendability of which British

Opposite:
Jimi Hendrix performing in London, 1967.

Tinted 'granny glasses' were a signature of hippie style.

fashion had become so representative – was surmounted by the industry's appropriation of the look. Hippies had rejected the very idea of the fashion designer, their early image coming not from the hand of any one person but evolving among themselves in manifestation of their vision of a better world; dress had political consequences, but it should also be enjoyed, without having to acquiesce in the dictates of designers as to how something should be worn and for how long. The fashion designer was all but redundant, according to the counterculture, and, while the hippie dream of equality was not without its ambiguities when it came to gender roles, such convictions did have some resonance with the burgeoning women's movement.

Hippie style was a significant shift from the clean modernity of Mary Quant, but was soon appropriated by many British designers, including Ossie Clark, Zandra Rhodes and Thea Porter. In particular, it was the interest in other cultures that was reflected in their work, in colourful prints that revealed the influence of the dress of diverse places and ethnicities. The signature style of Thea Porter was drawn from her having lived in the Middle East as a child. Porter's shop, in Greek Street, London, first specialised in imported Middle Eastern homewares, as well as antique caftans, which sold so successfully that Porter began to design them herself to meet customer demand. A loosely cut ankle-length garment, the caftan lent itself well to luxurious fabrics and opulent decoration. Porter claimed to 'hate clothes that look new', and her caftans, while certainly not faithful reproductions, embodied something of the spirit of the harem, and she gained an international name and a clientele that included many celebrities. Porter's evening dresses and kimonos were similarly made from silks, brocades and velvets, with detailed embroidery, while the fullness of gypsy dresses allowed her romantic imagination to explore fabrics that were increasingly elaborate in colour and pattern. Porter also dressed many male rock and pop stars, including members of the Beatles and the Rolling Stones, but also Donovan, whose image was often received in the media as a whimsical but comprehensible interpretation of hippie identity.

Opposite Granny Takes a Trip in World's End, Chelsea, Gandalf's Garden was a community based upon concepts of mysticism: a shop, cafe and centre for all things 'alternative', it promoted a restful ambience and advocated meditation rather

than drugs, and published a magazine of the same name. The shop was among the first of its kind in London and provided something of a template for other businesses that supported and catered for alternative lifestyles. In some sense, the impact of the counterculture in Britain had suggested a return to the influence of American culture, but enterprises such as Gandalf's Garden underlined discrete elements of native influence too, of a quintessential 'Englishness' that would be critical to the look of fashion in early-1970s Britain. However disjunctive these different worlds might have seemed, the way had been paved for the gingham and lace romanticism of designers such as Gina Fratini, and for the Edwardiana of Laura Ashley, who brought milkmaids and lace parasols to the British high street. Even Mary Quant had adapted to the new style, using Liberty Tana lawn prints in less structured ensembles, creating a very different vision of femininity to that with which she had begun the decade.

Opposite:
The 1968 psychedelic animated film *Yellow Submarine* was based on the music of the Beatles.

Hippies in
Piccadilly, 1969.
Hippie style in
particular blurred
the gender-specific
nature of fashion.

91

Conclusion

FASHION IN 1960s Britain wrought significant changes in social mores, and the innovations of the decade represent the incomparable ambitions of a generation. In its spirit of meritocracy, British style achieved a new international currency. But, more than any previous decade, the 1960s were constructed and scrutinised in the media, being branded while they progressed, and the epithets of 'swinging' and 'permissive' have endured, with fashions such as the mini-skirt still symbolic of the decade's youthful bravado and enormous social change. Subsequent critiques of the 1960s would focus on its consumerist hedonism, but Harold Macmillan's claim that 'most of our people have never had it so good' had indeed come with a clause that gave some forewarning of the troubles that would ail British society in future decades: 'What is beginning to worry some of us is "Is it too good to be true?" or perhaps I should say "Is it too good to last?"'

The mythologisation of the 1960s became more pronounced against the economic decline that Britain experienced in the 1970s, and the break with traditional

Opposite:
Diana Rigg starred in the James Bond film *On Her Majesty's Secret Service* in 1969, with an image markedly different from that of her earlier role as Emma Peel in *The Avengers*. The hippie aesthetic is here given an edge of glamour.

values that fashion had symbolised engendered much political conflict. When the first skinheads emerged in the latter years of the 1960s, their influences had been mod style, ska music and the West Indian rude boy. In the 1970s their image was inscribed with a contrary sense of hostility and aggression as it became the uniform of far-right nationalists.

While the distinction between youth and adulthood was made more complex by the changes of the 1960s – it was only in 1969 that the age for voting was reduced to eighteen, yet until 1972 it was still possible to leave school at fourteen and seek employment – young people's lives had been forever changed by that culture. The affluence of the 1960s diminished certain class distinctions and expanded the opportunities of future generations. The cultural and social upheaval of the decade still resonates, and its images of libertine youth continue to be subject to both pastiche and parody in contemporary popular culture and fashion.

Further Reading

Breward, Christopher; Gilbert, David; and Lister, Jenny (editors). *Swinging Sixties: Fashion in London and Beyond 1955–1970.* V&A, 2006.

Décharné, Max. *King's Road: The Rise and Fall of the Hippest Street in the World.* Phoenix, 2006.

Donnelly, Mark. *Sixties Britain: Culture, Society and Politics.* Longman, 2005.

Fogg, Marnie. *Boutique: a '60s Cultural Phenomenon.* Mitchell Beazley, 2003.

Hewitt, Paolo. *Fab Gear: the Beatles and Fashion.* Prestel, 2011.

Lester, Richard. *Photographing Fashion: British Style in the Sixties.* ACC Editions, 2009.

Levy, Shawn. *Ready, Steady, Go! The Smashing Rise and Giddy Fall of Swinging London.* Broadway Books, 2003.

Reed, Paula. *Fifty Fashion Looks that Changed the 1960s.* Conran, 2012.

Ross, Geoffrey Aquilina. *Day of the Peacock: Style for Men 1963-1973.* V&A, 2011.

Walford, Jonathan. *Sixties Fashion: From 'Less is More' to Youthquake.* Thomas & Hudson, 2013.

Index

19 magazine 18
Alfie (film) 59
Androgynous fashions 36, 70–1, 81, 90–1
Anello & Davide 31
Ashley, Laura 89
Austin Reed 53
Ayton, Sylvia 54
Bacon, Francis 85
Bailey, David *16*, 17, 18, 61, *62*, 63–4, 66, 67
Bazaar boutique 6, *42*, 43
Beatles, the 21, 23, 29, *29*, 30, 33, *33*, 35, 47, 66, 87; *A Hard Day's Night* (film) 31, 66; Apple Boutique *32*, 35; mop-top haircut 31; *Sgt. Pepper's Lonely Hearts Club Band* 31; *Yellow Submarine* (film) 81, *88*–9
Bedazzled (film) 66
Beehive hairstyle 27
Best, George 15, *15*
Biba 18, 21, 25, 45, *46*, 60
Birtwell, Celia 47
Blake, Peter 31
Blow Up (film) 66, *68*–9
Body-painting 82
Booker, Christopher 73
Boutiques 43, 50, 53, 54, 57
British Home Stores 25
Burton 53
Butterick 45

C&A 53
Caftan 87
Caine, Michael 59
Carnaby Street 7, 10, 36, 39, 47–8, *49*, 50, 67
Carter, Ernestine 43
Christie, Julie 57
Clark, Ossie 47, 54, 86
Class mobility 12–13, 15, 19, 21, 67
Conran, Terence 12
Consumer culture 7, 9, 12–13, 18–19, 41, 48, 73, 77, 85, 92
Contraceptive pill 18, 67
Cream 82, *83*
Daily Mirror 18–19
Dannimac Rainwear 25
Darling (film) 66
Delaney, Shelagh 17
Deneuve, Catherine 66
Denny, Robyn 53
Denza, Vanessa 44
Dickinson, Geoffrey 59, 60
Donovan 23, 87
Donovan, Terence 61, 63
Doors 83
Duffy, Brian 61, 63
Dylan, Bob 82
Easy Rider (film) 80
Epstein, Brian 31
Esquire magazine 71
Flares 81

Foale and Tuffin 17, 48, 54, *58*
Fordyce, Keith 25
Fratini, Gina 89
Gandalf's Garden 87, 89
Georgy Girl (film) 66
Ginsberg, Allen 73
'Granny' glasses 31, 81, *86*
Granny Takes a Trip 50, 60, 85, 87
Grateful Dead 82
Hair (musical) 81
Halasz, Piri 60
Harrison, George 35
Harrods 6, 44
Hemmings, David 66
Hendrix, Jimi 23–4, 50, 82, *85*
Hippies *74*, 75, 78, 79, 80–1, *80*, 82, *82*, 85, 86, *86*, 87, 90–*1*
Hockney, David 47
Holtom, Gerald 77
Home dressmaking 45, 57
Honey magazine 18, 54
Hulanicki, Barbara 45, *46*, 47
Hung On You 50, 76, 85
Hunt, Marsha 81
I Was Lord Kitchener's Valet 48, 50, *51*
Incredible String Band 78, *80*
Isle of Wight Festival 82
Jaeger 53
Jagger, Mick 35, 36, 50, 66
Jefferson Airplane 82
Jones, Brian 36

Joplin, Janis 81
Juste, Samantha 27
Keeler, Christine 15
King's Road 6, *9*, 36, 43, 50
Kinks, the 39, *39*, 48
Knightsbridge 44
Leary, Timothy 80, 81
Lee Cooper 25
Lennon, John 29, 31, 35, 50, 73, 77, 81
Life magazine 71
London 6, *8*, 23, 27, *32*, 35, 43, *46*, 47, 48, *49*, 50, *51*, *52*, 53, 57, 59–61, 64, 66–7, 71, 73, 76, 79, 85, 87, 89, *90–1*
Lord John 48, *52*, 53
Macmillan, Harold 10, 92
Magazines 18, 38–9
Marks & Spencer 53
McGowan, Cathy *24*, 25, 27
McNair, Archie 43
Melody Maker 36
Merc 48
Military tailoring 31, 81
Miller, Roger 60
Millings, Dougie 29
Mini (car) *38*, 59
Mini-skirt *7*, 21, 25, 45, 64, 67, 85, 92
Miss Selfridge 54
Mitchell, Joni 82
Mods *6*, 21, 23, 27, 29, *37*, 93
Moore, Roger 48
Moraes, Henrietta 85
Morris, William 85
Mr Fish 36, 50
New Musical Express 36
Nicholson, Viv 13
Nureyev, Rudolf 66

Oldham, Andrew 35
Ono, Yoko 77
Op Art 45, *46*, 47
Palisades 50
Paper dresses 12, 54
Parkinson, Norman 61
'Peacock' style 39, *39*, 48
Petticoat magazine 18
Plunkett-Greene, Alexander 43
Pollock, Alice 47
Porter, Thea 86, 87
Portobello Market 50
Profumo scandal 15
Prudence and the Pill (film) 66
Psychedelia 31, *32*, *33*, 50, *52*, 80, 81
Quant, Mary 6, 7, 10, 17, 21, *42*, 43–5, *44*, *45*, 50, 54, 57, 59, 82, 86, 89
Queen magazine *9*, 17, *17*, 71
Quorum 47
Ready Steady Go! 23, *24*, 25, 27, *28*, 29, 36
Realist cinema 17, 66
Redgrave, Lynn 67
Rhodes, Zandra 54, 86
Richard, Cliff 23, 29
Rigg, Diana *93*
Rolfe, Colin 64
Rolling Stones, the 23, *34*, 35, 48, 87
Royal College of Art 44
Sassoon, Vidal 45
Saturday Night and Sunday Morning (film) 17
Scotty's model agency 48
Sexual freedom 15, 67, 77
Shaw, Sandie 23, 27
Shrimpton, Jean *16*, 17, *17*, 18, 63–4, *63*, *65*, 66, 67

Simpsons of Piccadilly 53
Skin-heads 93
Small Faces, the 48
Smashing Time (film) 66
Springfield, Dusty 25, *26*, 27
Stamp, Terence *65*, 66
Stephen, John 47–8, 50
Stern, Bert 71
Sunday Times 18, 43, 44, 61
Synthetic fabrics *19*, 53, *55*, *56*, 85
Taste of Honey, A (film) 17
Teddy boy 6, 12, 29
Teenager 18–19
The Fool (design collective) 35
The Italian Job (film) 66
The Knack … and How to Get It (film) 66, *70*
Tie-dye 78
Time magazine 59–60, 71
Top of the Pops 27
Topshop 54
Townshend, Pete 36
Tree, Penelope 57
Tushingham, Rita 67
Twiggy 6, 7, 25, 54, 57, 67, 70–1, *72*
Union Jack flag 36, *38*, 59
Vince menswear 47
Vogue (American) 60
Vogue (British) 17, 63, 64, 70
Vreeland, Diana 60
Warhol, Andy 66
Watts, Charlie 36
Who, The *28*, 29, 36, *37*, 48, 59, 82
Wickham, Vicki 25
Wilson, Harold 21, 59
Wolfe, Tom 80
Woodstock festival 82
Woollands 44